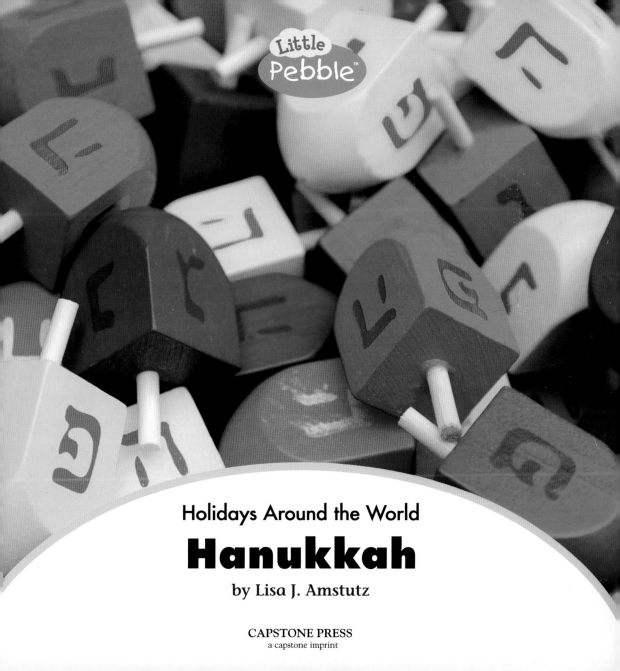

Little Pebble™

Holidays Around the World

Hanukkah

by Lisa J. Amstutz

CAPSTONE PRESS
a capstone imprint

Little Pebble is published by Capstone Press,
1710 Roe Crest Drive, North Mankato, Minnesota 56003
www.mycapstone.com

Library of Congress Cataloging-in-Publication Data
Names: Amstutz, Lisa J., author.
Title: Hanukkah / by Lisa J. Amstutz.
Description: North Mankato, Minnesota : Capstone Press, 2017. | Series: Little pebble.
  Holidays around the world | K to grade 3, ages 5-7. | Includes bibliographical
  references and index.
Identifiers: LCCN 2016034433 | ISBN 9781515748540 (library binding) | ISBN
  9781515748601 (paperback) | ISBN 9781515748786 (eBook PDF)
Subjects: LCSH: Hanukkah—Juvenile literature.
Classification: LCC BM695.H3 A695 2017 | DDC 296.4/35—dc23
LC record available at https://lccn.loc.gov/2016034433

Editorial Credits
Jill Kalz, editor; Julie Peters, designer; Pam Mitsakos, media researcher;
Steve Walker, production specialist

Photo Credits
Shutterstock: AlbertBuchatskyy, 3, Anastazzo, 9, Arina P Habich, 15, ChameleonsEye,
11, 13, GreenArt Photography, 16, ifong, 8, Karaidel, cover, Lisa F. Young, 5, liza1979, 1,
22, 24, back cover, Maglara, 17, Sean Locke Photography, 21, SLdesign, design element,
tomertu, 7; Thinkstock: arinahabich, 19

Printed and bound in China
PO7884LEOS17

Table of Contents

What Is It?

Lights glow.

Hanukkah is here!

Hanukkah is in November or December. It lasts eight days.

The Story

Long ago a lamp was lit.

It had only a bit of oil.

But it burned for eight days.

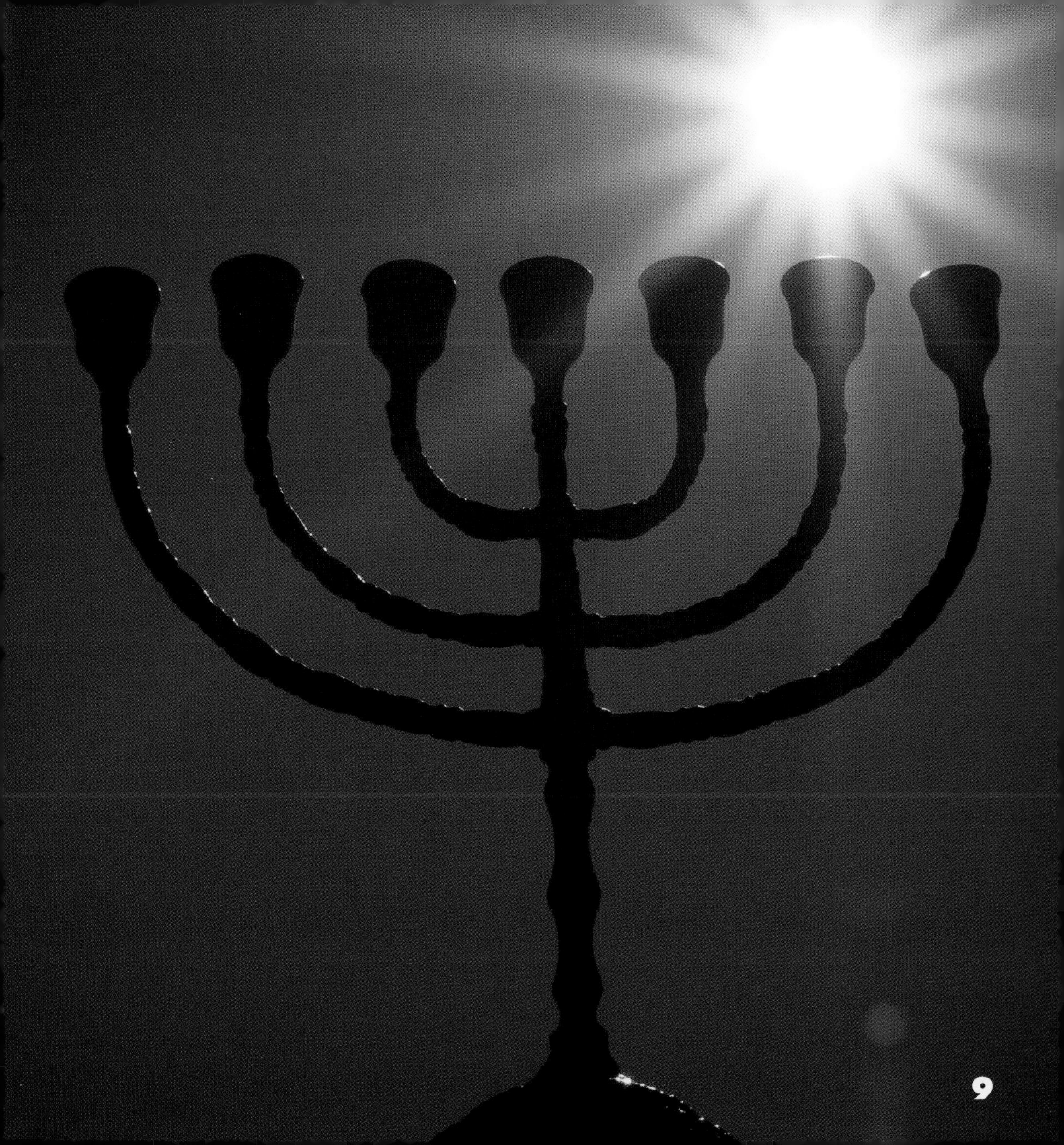

How did the lamp stay lit?

No one knows.

It was a gift from God!

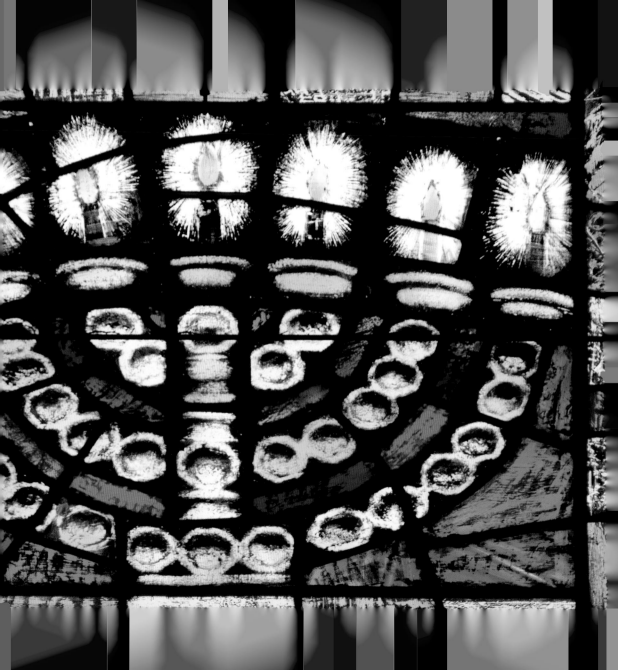

Time of Joy

Families pray.

They light candles.

They light one each night.

People give gifts.

They give money.

Some money is candy.

People fry latkes
and donuts in oil.
The donuts have jelly
inside. Yum!

Kids play games.

They spin a top.

It has four sides.

It is a happy time!

Glossary

Hanukkah—a Jewish holiday; Jews follow the religion of Judaism

latke—a potato pancake

oil—a slippery liquid that does not mix with water

pray—to speak to God and give thanks

Read More

Herrington, Lisa M. *Hanukkah.* Rookie Read-About Holidays. New York: Children's Press, 2014.

Keogh, Josie. *Hanukkah.* Happy Holidays! New York: PowerKids Press, 2013.

Lawrence, Elizabeth. *Celebrate Hanukkah.* Bookworms: Our Holidays. New York: Cavendish Square Publishing, 2016.

Internet Sites

FactHound offers a safe, fun way to find Internet sites related to this book. All of the sites on FactHound have been researched by our staff.

Here's all you do:
Visit *www.facthound.com*
Type in this code: 9781515748540

Check out projects, games and lots more at
www.capstonekids.com

Critical Thinking Using the Common Core

1. Name three things people may do during Hanukkah. (Key Ideas and Details)

2. How many candles are lit each night during Hanukkah? (Key Ideas and Details)

Index